COMING SOON

What does the *Book of Revelation* say for today's followers of Christ?

Pre-order now at **michaeljchanley.com**

Basic Christianity: Foundations of Faith for Following Jesus Today

Published in the United States by Churchlit Publishing.

Author: Michael J. Chanley
Editor: Laura Meyer
Cover Design: Michael J. Chanley

Paperback ISBN:	979-8-9892277-6-1
Ebook/Digital ASIN:	B0GHZWSWHY

Subjects: Christianity, Jesus Christ, New Testament, Faith, Love, Basics, Introduction, Christian Living, Spiritual Formation, Gospel, Religion, Christian Church

Bulk sales discounts may be available. To inquire, please contact sales@churchlit.com. For speaking engagements, email: office@michaeljchanley.com.

Basic Christianity Series

Explore a series designed to help readers understand, live, and grow in the Christian faith with clarity and confidence. Written for those who are new to faith, returning after time away, or seeking a deeper foundation, each book focuses on the core teachings of Scripture and what it means to follow Jesus in everyday life.

Rather than assuming prior knowledge, the series invites honest questions, encourages thoughtful discussion, and emphasizes faith that is lived out in love, community, and service. Some volumes explore foundational beliefs, others study individual books of the Bible, and future titles address real questions people ask about their faith.

Together, the ***Basic Christianity*** series offers a grounded, accessible pathway for individuals, small groups, and churches to grow in faith and follow Jesus more faithfully, one step at a time.

visit **michaeljchanley.com**

Also by Michael J. Chanley

God Called Love: Experience Love In An Anxious World Needing Grace

Experiencing God Called Love: 5 Week Journal on God's Love & Spiritual Practices Guidebook

Hope & Honeybess: Lessons of Faith From a Local Beekeeper

Escape: The Traps of Christianity

Escape: The Traps of Christianity Journal

Chasing WHALES: A Spiritual Dive with Jonah

Collaborate: Family + Church

The Art of Parenting: Nurturing Happy, Confident, and Resilient Children

Also from Michael J. Chanley

Books with Journals

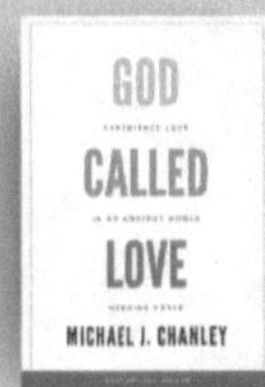

Topical Studies

Basic Christianity Series

Coming soon

Learn more at
michaeljchanley.com

Basic Christianity

Foundations of Faith for Following Jesus Today

Michael J. Chanley

For Rose.
Thank you for a lifetime of love.

Contents

Prologue: Beginning the Journey

Christianity can feel complicated, but at its core, it is about understanding God, His love, and His work in our lives. This book is an exploration of the essentials: the foundational questions that shape our faith.

We begin with the Bible, not simply as a collection of writings, but as a testament to the life, death, and resurrection of Jesus Christ. The four Gospels stand at the center of Scripture, revealing God's love in action and guiding us in how to live. Those who experienced Jesus' life and teachings wanted to obey Him and to share what they had learned with others.

Next, we ask, "Who is God?" God is one, yet revealed in three persons: Father, Son, and Holy Spirit. His character is unified, and His love is perfect. Understanding God helps us see the path He has laid before us and the way He works in the world.

We also confront the ultimate question: "What happens when I die?" There is a heaven and a hell, and each of us has a choice. Because all have sinned and fallen short of God's glory, salvation is necessary. But salvation is not only about eternity, it transforms our lives here and now, affecting our relationships, our families, and our communities.

Then comes the practical question: "What must I do to be saved?" The Bible outlines a clear path: hear God's Word, believe in Jesus, confess our sins, repent, and be baptized. These steps lead to eternal life, but they also invite God's love to reshape our hearts, our actions, and our communities. Salvation is both personal and communal, touching every area of life.

Finally, we ask, "What does it mean to be a Christian?" Christianity is not a label or an identity imposed by others. Rather, it is a life submitted to Christ. To be a Christian is to live as a slave of God, walking in His ways, following His example, and allowing His love to guide every decision. It is to die to ourselves, love others unconditionally, and serve those who are hurting or lost.

Ultimately, this book is about alignment, alignment with God, His Word, and His Church. It is a guide for understanding who God is, recognizing our need for salvation, and choosing to follow Him in every area of life. By the end of these pages, my hope is that you will not only understand these essentials, but live them, share them, and see God's love at work through your life and in your community.

Welcome to the journey of basic Christianity.

"In fact, everyone who wants to live a godly life in Christ Jesus will be persecuted, while evildoers and impostors will go from bad to worse, deceiving and being deceived. But as for you, continue in what you have learned and have become convinced of, because you know those from whom you learned it, and how from infancy you have known the Holy Scriptures, which are able to make you wise for salvation through faith in Christ Jesus. All Scripture is God-breathed and is useful for teaching, rebuking, correcting and training in righteousness, so that the servant of God may be thoroughly equipped for every good work." [1]

— 2 Timothy 3:12-17

Four Accounts

The Moment That Changed Everything

The martyrs of the first century did not die for the Bible. They did not die for freedom to practice their own religion. They did not die over political affiliations or because someone posted something they didn't like on social media.

They died because of an incredible thing that happened through Jesus Christ.

And their witness of Jesus' life, teachings, death, burial, and resurrection is the main thing. Once we begin to understand who Jesus was, it changes us. It may even revolutionize the way we live, if we allow it to do so.

[1] *The New International Version*. (2011). (2 Ti 3:10–17). Grand Rapids, MI: Zondervan.

Most people know some stories from the Bible. Many have parts of it memorized. I recently spoke with someone who told me she has read the entire Bible thirty-seven times. She reads two chapters every morning and two every evening. That is an incredible act of sincere devotion.

We are blessed to live in a world where we have ready access to God's Word. Many of us have read all or part of the Bible. However, not many of us truly know the story of the Bible. That raises an important question: why do we have the Bible at all? Why does it exist?

Understanding the basic story of the Bible strengthens our faith. It girds us for battle. It solidifies the ground on which we stand. It also shapes how we read the Bible and how we apply it to our lives.

Some may say, "The Bible is just confusing. I can't understand it."

In reality, the Bible is an easy book to understand. I would argue it is easier to understand than learning the rules of driving a car, or figuring out how to use a smart device or a computer.

Søren Kierkegaard, the nineteenth-century philosopher and theologian, once wrote:

"The matter is quite simple. The Bible is very easy to understand. But we Christians are a bunch of scheming swindlers. We pretend to be unable to understand it because we know very well that the minute we understand, we are obliged to act accordingly… Christian scholarship is the Church's prodigious invention to defend itself against the Bible… Dreadful it is to fall into the hands of the living God. Yes it is even dreadful to be alone with the New Testament."[2]

— Søren Kierkegaard, Provocations: Spiritual Writings of Kierkegaard

---

[2] Kierkegaard, Soren. *Provocations: Spiritual Writings of Kierkegaard.* Plough Publishing House 2014., 2014.

That is a harsh criticism, but his point is worth hearing. The Bible is easier to understand, especially when we understand how it came to exist. The hard work is not comprehension; the hard work is application. It requires discipline to live out what Scripture reveals, holding it up as a mirror and seeing ourselves measured against the likeness of Christ.

One of the reasons biblical understanding is so often lacking is the absence of biblically grounded teaching. Many churches do not teach the Bible as it is written. Instead, they begin with a self-help message and then search the Scriptures to support it. Others try to craft a message that simply leaves people feeling good about themselves.

But reading and understanding the Bible does not usually make us feel good about ourselves. In fact, my hope is often the opposite. When we are exposed to the truth of Scripture, it should unsettle us. To realize that God loves us so deeply that He died for our sins—and to confront our pride, greed, lust, selfishness, and rebellion—ought to humble us. It is difficult to feel comfortable in the presence of that truth unless we choose to ignore it.

In the Book of James, there is a passage that speaks to this very sentiment:

"Do not merely listen to the word, and so deceive yourselves. Do what it says. Anyone who listens to the word but does not do what it says is like someone who looks at his face in a mirror and, after looking at himself, goes away and immediately forgets what he looks like. But whoever looks intently into the perfect law that gives freedom, and continues in it—not forgetting what they have heard, but doing it—they will be blessed in what they do." [3]

—James 1:22-25

[3] Ibid. Jas 1:22–25.

So why do we get this wrong so often? Why do we read Jesus' words about compassion, love, and mercy, yet conduct our lives with harshness, greed, and manipulation?

Part of the problem, as pastor Andy Stanley has said, is this: many of us know stories from the Bible, but we do not know the story of the Bible.

Knowing the story of how the Bible came to be helps us move from merely listening to the Word to actually doing it. It strengthens our faith and reshapes how we approach Scripture. It reveals just how relevant and transformative this book truly is.

The Beginning of the Story

The Bible begins with Genesis, but the story of the Bible begins in Luke 1. This is a passage we may read often without fully appreciating its significance.

"Many have undertaken to draw up an account of the things that have been fulfilled among us, just as they were handed down to us by those who from the first were eyewitnesses and servants of the word. With this in mind, since I myself have carefully investigated everything from the beginning, I too decided to write an orderly account for you, most excellent Theophilus, so that you may know the certainty of the things you have been taught." [4]

— *Luke 1:1-4*

[4] Ibid. Lk 1:1–4.

Luke, a physician and likely the only non-Jewish author of any Biblical text, sits down to write about something extraordinary that has just happened. He notes that "many" had already attempted to record these events. As a careful historian, Luke gathers eyewitness testimony to produce an accurate account. He later writes a second letter to Theophilus, the book of Acts, for the same reason.

As Andy Stanley has pointed out, Luke did not know he was writing the Bible when he wrote this letter.

Writing in the ancient world was expensive, time-consuming, and labor-intensive. For Luke to write, and for his work to be copied and distributed, meant something remarkable had occurred. Luke takes note that others had also made an attempt to account for what had happened and, in so doing, records for us the beginnings of the origin of the Bible we know and love.

Why, though, would there be others who had aspired to write down an account of the things that had happened? Well, the origin story of the Bible hinges on a single moment that transformed the world and it is the moment that answers the "Why" question.

That moment is recorded in Luke 23 and 24.

In Luke 23, we read about Jesus brutal death on the cross. Then, a very dead Jesus is placed in a tomb. Luke writes about the moment when the women prepare spices and perfumes. Why? Because Jesus was dead. Truly dead. No one expected Him to return. His followers were scattered, disillusioned, and afraid.

Jesus was completely dead. All of His followers were in a state of despair.

There were undoubtedly no Christians when Jesus died. For one, the term hadn't been coined yet. Secondly, all of His disciples had deserted Him, denied Him, and betrayed Him. They had no Bible to look back and explain what had happened. Jesus' earliest followers were living the story in real time.

Then, we read about the most pivotal moment in human history. Luke 24 records the resurrection of Jesus. When the women arrive at the tomb to honor the grave of the dead Jesus, they are shocked to find it empty. Moreso, a heavenly messenger is there and asks them a pivotal question.

"... 'Why do you look for the living among the dead? [6] He is not here; he has risen! Remember how he told you, while he was still with you in Galilee: 'The Son of Man must be delivered over to the hands of sinners, be crucified and on the third day be raised again.' " Then they remembered his words." [5]

— Luke 25:5b-8

"Why do you look for the living among the dead? He is not here; he has risen!"

This is the moment that changed everything.

The risen Jesus appeared to His followers and began to teach them again, now with understanding that could only come after seeing His resurrection fulfilled. It is Jesus' victory over death that made all of the difference.

Why the Bible Exists

[5] Ibid. Lk 24:5–8.

When Luke writes that "many have undertaken" to record these events, history confirms his claim. Early Christian writings were widely circulated, copied, hidden, and often destroyed. Christians were persecuted by both Jewish and Roman authorities.

The Jews rejected Jesus as Messiah. The Romans rejected Christianity because it challenged their worship of power and control. Christians proclaimed allegiance to a risen King, which Rome perceived as a threat. Christ was competition to their ruthless rule.

Yet despite persecution, the writings that survived became the four Gospels and the rest of the New Testament. The early Christians endured not because books were being burned, but because Jesus had been raised from the dead.

No resurrection means no Bible.

The Gospels exist because Jesus lived, was crucified, and rose again. Paul's letters exist because the apostles could not help but tell others what they had seen. They were willing to suffer and die because of that moment.

Centuries later, when persecution ceased, believers gathered these writings, recognized their authenticity, and preserved both the New Testament and the Old Testament as one unified story. A story centered on Christ.

The Bible was handed down to us not to win arguments, justify cruelty, or inflate our pride. It was given to change us. To form us into people who live lives worthy of the calling we have received.

It was given to us to help us follow in the Way of Jesus Christ.

What is the Bible?

At the heart of Christian faith is a simple but essential question: *What is the Bible?* More personally, *what is the Bible to you?*

The Bible is God's Word, authored through His people, telling the story of how He rescues humanity from sin. It is hope. It is transformation. It is a tool in the hands of believers.

Like any tool, it can be misused. History shows us that Scripture has been weaponized to justify evil. But God's Word was never meant to harm. It was given to heal, restore, and shape us into the likeness of Christ.

As followers of Christ, we believe that the Bible is God's Word, given through and alongside God's people. It tells the story of all that God has done to rescue humanity from sin. It is a collection of books, letters, poems, and histories that together bear witness to God's redemptive work in the world. It offers hope, shapes belief, and, when rightly understood, transforms those who receive it.

Importantly, the Bible is not only something we read; it is something that forms us. In the hands of believers, it becomes a resource that equips us to love one another, to serve faithfully, and to remain united despite the persistent efforts of the enemy to divide and destroy.

One helpful way to understand the Bible is to see it as a powerful instrument. Military pilots and tank operators are trained to understand that the machines they operate are not the weapon, they are. The aircraft or tank becomes an extension of the one operating it. In the same way, Scripture functions as a powerful instrument in the hands of the believer. The Word itself is good, but its impact depends on the heart, intent, and faithfulness of the one who wields it.

History reminds us of this sobering reality. Scripture has been misused and distorted to justify horrific evil. African peoples were dehumanized in early American history by pastors who manipulated Scripture to defend slavery. Indigenous nations across the Americas were devastated as God's Word was weaponized by colonial powers to sanctify greed and violence. Women have been subjected to abuse by those who twisted God's Word to support misogyny.

Even beyond the Western world, the pattern of abusing scripture persists. In sixteenth-century Japan, the warlord Oda Nobunaga initially welcomed Christian missionaries, not for their faith, but for their military technology and the perceived fearlessness Christianity instilled in warriors. When political power shifted, Christianity was violently suppressed. Missionaries were executed, believers were forced to renounce their faith, and the church was driven underground for nearly three centuries. When Japan eventually reopened to the world, only a remnant of believers remained—faithful, but hidden. [6]

These stories do not require rewriting history. They require learning from it.

God's Word was never intended to be a weapon for oppression, domination, or harm. It is meant to be a means of grace. It is an instrument for doing good, not evil. The difference in how it is used lies in the faithfulness and intentions of each of us.

The Bible consistently calls God's people toward love: love for the orphan and the widow, the hungry and the poor, the outsider and the broken. It calls us to die to ourselves, to reject pride and power, and to be shaped into the likeness of Christ. When Scripture is rightly received, it does not harden hearts; it softens them. It does not divide for the sake of dominance; it reconciles for the sake of redemption.

As this chapter closes, the question remains not only *what the Bible is*, but *how it will be held.* In humility and obedience, God's Word becomes life-giving. In arrogance and self-interest, it

---

[6] Larson, Eugene. *Japanese Ban Christian Missionaries* | Research Starters | EBSCO Research. Accessed January 29, 2026. https://www.ebsco.com.

becomes destructive. The difference lies not in the text itself, but in the posture of the one who opens it.

As Paul reminds his young mentee, Timothy:

"But as for you, continue in what you have learned and have become convinced of, because you know those from whom you learned it, and how from infancy you have known the Holy Scriptures, which are able to make you wise for salvation through faith in Christ Jesus. All Scripture is God-breathed and is useful for teaching, rebuking, correcting and training in righteousness, so that the servant of God may be thoroughly equipped for every good work." [7]

— 2 Timothy 3:14–17

Scripture equips us for every good work. When we understand the story of how the Bible came to be, it changes how we read it and, ultimately, how we apply it to our lives.

Knowing what the Bible is to us, personally, allows us to see it as a tool for following Christ in His perfect love.

Discussion Questions:

- How did you first discover the story of the Bible?
- What is one of your favorite stories from the Bible?
- How does knowing the story of the Bible strengthen your faith in Jesus?

[7] The New International Version (Grand Rapids, MI: Zondervan, 2011), 2 Ti 3:14–17.

"Jesus answered, 'I am the way and the truth and the life. No one comes to the Father except through me. If you really know me, you will know my Father as well. From now on, you do know him and have seen him.'" [8]

— John 14:6-7

Three Persons

Who Is God?

In the previous chapter, we explored the story of the Bible. We learned that we have a Bible because Jesus' followers heard what He said, saw what He did, witnessed His life, witnessed His death, and then, miraculously, saw Him alive again after His resurrection.

Those who experienced what Jesus said and did wanted to obey what He told them to do. Because of that, they wrote to others and endured tremendous persecution so His story could be told. And we should never forget this: because of their faithfulness, today we can know His story and tell it to others.

We asked the question, What is the Bible? We said that the Bible is God's Word, co-authored with God's people (His followers) to tell us what God has done to rescue us from our sins. It is hope for all mankind. It is a collection of books, letters, writings, and stories that transform us. Importantly, the Bible is a tool, even a weapon, in the hands of the believer. Not a instrument for violence, rather, it is one that equips us to serve and love one another despite the enemy's efforts to destroy and divide.

We have the Bible today because of one miraculous moment: Jesus lived, taught, fulfilled prophecy, died, and

[8] Ibid. Jn 14:6–7.

then—this is the moment upon which everything hinges—He was resurrected. Without the resurrection, there is no Bible.

Had He not risen from the grave, there would have been no point whatsoever in writing down the deeds and teachings of Jesus. To understand who Jesus is, however, we have to ask a deeper question.

This chapter asks a new question: Who is God?

You may have attended church your entire life. You may have accepted Jesus Christ as your Lord and Savior. You may have experienced the gifts of the Holy Spirit. And yet, you may still struggle to answer this question.

Who is God?

If that is you, do not feel alone. You are not the only one.

To understand how we arrived at our understanding of who God is, we must first understand the story of how the Bible came to be. We must choose to believe, with faith, in what it says. Then we can look back, far back in history, to see how God revealed Himself to His people.

Constantine and a Turning Point in History

In the early fourth century, a power struggle erupted among the rulers of Rome. It culminated in a confrontation between two emperors: Maxentius and Constantine. On October 28, 312 AD, their armies met north of Rome at what became known as the Battle of the Milvian Bridge.

The Milvian Bridge crossed the Tiber River. Maxentius positioned his forces on the north side of the river, hoping to stop Constantine before he could cross and reach Rome. Constantine was outnumbered. Historians estimate his army numbered around 20,000 soldiers, while Maxentius commanded at least 25,000 (possibly as many as 100,000).

According to historical accounts, Constantine saw a vision of a cross in the sky above the sun, accompanied by the words

In hoc signo vinces: "In this sign you will conquer." [9] Constantine did not fully understand the vision at first. Many in Rome worshiped the sun god (Sol) and the sky god (Jupiter). Later, in a dream, Christ appeared to Constantine and instructed him to place the symbol of the cross on his soldiers' shields.

The next day, Constantine led his army into battle, under the banner of Christ, and decisively defeated Maxentius. He entered Rome the following day. Constantine converted to Christianity, and in 313 AD issued the Edict of Milan, ending the persecution of Christians throughout the Roman Empire. Ten years later, in 323 AD, Christianity became the official religion of Rome. [10] [11]

For the first time, believers were able to come out of hiding. Scholars gathered to examine the writings about Jesus. Councils such as the one arranged at Nicaea convened to establish unity in teaching, filter out false doctrines, and protect the Church from groups attempting to distort the truth. The result was the Bible in its present form: sixty-six books written by forty authors, recognized and affirmed in the fourth century.

As leaders studied Scripture, they faced a new challenge. How do you explain who God is to a people who had lived in a polytheistic culture?

One God, Revealed as Three

Roman culture accepted many gods. People worshiped anything they believed held power. Sailors sacrificed to the god

---

[9] Templar Cross. "In Signo Hoc Vinces: Meaning and Origin." July 31, 2020. https://templar-cross.com/blogs/knights-templar-blog/in-signo-hoc-vinces.

[10] Hudson, M. "Battle of Milvian Bridge." Encyclopedia Britannica, October 21, 2025. https://www.britannica.com/topic/Battle-of-the-Milvian-Bridge.

[11] Kings & Generals Channel on YouTube. *Milvian Bridge 312 - Rise of Christianity DOCUMENTARY.* Accessed January 30, 2026. https://www.youtube.com/watch?v=VbFtMXytMj8.

of the sea. Warriors sacrificed to gods of war. Farmers honored ancestors or earth gods to ensure a good harvest.

Into this worldview came the Christian proclamation: God is one.

And yet Scripture speaks of the Father, the Son, and the Holy Spirit. So who is God?

This question led the early Church to articulate what we now call the Trinity. The word "Trinity" does not appear in the Bible, but the truth it describes is found throughout Scripture and is central to Christian faith.

The Trinity is the doctrine explaining the fullness of God as Father, Son, and Holy Spirit: three persons, one God. God is not divided into parts, nor does He merely appear in different forms. Each person of the Trinity is fully and completely God.

Harold Lindsell and Charles J. Woodbridge write:

"The mind of man cannot fully understand the mystery of the Trinity. He who has tried to understand the mystery fully will lose his mind; but he who would deny the Trinity will lose his soul."
—A Handbook of Christian Truth (1953), pp. 51–52 [12]

The Trinity is a mystery accepted by faith.
God the Father is fully God.
God the Son is fully God.
God the Holy Spirit is fully God.

During my years as a children's pastor, occasionally a child would ask a very profound question: "How can God be three persons and still One God?" It is a great question and one that is not easily answered. One of the best ways I found to explain it came from using a helpful illustration.

Consider, for the sake of simplicity, yourself as the center of the illustration. You are a person with multiple identies, you are a

[12] Sanders, Fred. "Who Said 'The Trinity: Try to Understand It, and You'll Lose Your Mind'?" The Scriptorium Daily, August 30, 2009. https://scriptoriumdaily.com/who-said-the-trinity-try-to-understand-it-and-youll-lose-your-mind.

child, a friend, and a neighbor. These are all different relationships, yet contained within the same person. If I submit myself into the illustration, I am a father, a husband, and a pastor. I am one person; yet, I represent myself in different ways, at unique moments, depending on the situation.

Or, another illustration that is also helpful, consider a pie cut into three slices: each slice is fully pie, made of the same substance. It is one pie, but served to three individuals or at three unique moments.

These examples, or illustrations, undoubtedly fall short if pressed too far, but they can help us begin to grasp the idea of how the Trinity exists.

As a beginner, defining the Trinity is far less important than understanding why it matters. It matters because it helps us take a step closer to experiencing the fullness of God.

Growing Into the Fullness of God

Paul addresses the unfathomable, yet approachable, nature of God's fullness as he recounts his prayers on our behalf:

"For this reason I kneel before the Father, from whom every family in heaven and on earth derives its name. I pray that out of his glorious riches he may strengthen you with power through his Spirit in your inner being, so that Christ may dwell in your hearts through faith. And I pray that you, being rooted and established in love, may have power, together with all the Lord's holy people, to grasp how wide and long and high and deep is the love of Christ, and to know this love that surpasses knowledge—that you may be filled to the measure of all the fullness of God.

Now to him who is able to do immeasurably more than all we ask or imagine, according to his power that is at work within us, to him be glory in the church and in Christ Jesus throughout all generations, for ever and ever! Amen." [13]

— Ephesians 3:14–21

Paul prays that believers would be filled "to the measure of all the fullness of God." The original Greek word for fullness is used here and its meaning is completion, fulfillment, or being made whole. [14] Growing into the fullness of God means we become more completely who we were designed to become.

This same word and concept appears as fulfillment in Romans 13:10, where Paul writes: "*Love does no harm to a neighbor. Therefore love is the fulfillment of the law.*" [15]

Another place we see this idea of fullness expanded on is in Colossians:

---

[13] *The New International Version* (Grand Rapids, MI: Zondervan, 2011), Eph 3:14–21.

[14] Strong, J. (2009). *A Concise Dictionary of the Words in the Greek Testament and The Hebrew Bible* (Vol. 1, p. 58). Bellingham, WA: Logos Bible Software.

[15] *The New International Version* (Grand Rapids, MI: Zondervan, 2011), Ro 13:10.

"So then, just as you received Christ Jesus as Lord, continue to live your lives in him, rooted and built up in him, strengthened in the faith as you were taught, and overflowing with thankfulness.

See to it that no one takes you captive through hollow and deceptive philosophy, which depends on human tradition and the elemental spiritual forces of this world rather than on Christ.

For in Christ all the fullness of the Deity lives in bodily form, and in Christ you have been brought to fullness. He is the head over every power and authority." [16]

— *Colossians 2:6–10*

Understanding the fullness of God is possible only through knowing the Father, in the name of the Son, and through the Holy Spirit. When we pray, we pray to the Father, through the Son, by the Spirit. In doing so, we participate in the fullness of who God is as He has revealed Himself.

These concepts are not something to be legalistic about. Forgetting a phrase in prayer is not a failure of faith. But if we want to grow spiritually, understanding who God is (Father, Son, and Holy Spirit) serves to deepen our relationship with Him. He is One; yet, His fullness is revealed to us in different ways.

Who Do You Say That I Am?

This brings us back to the central question of this chapter: Who is God?

More personally: Who do you believe God is?

Do you know Him? Jesus asked His disciples this very question in Matthew's Gospel:

[16] Ibid. Col 2:6–10.

"But what about you?" he asked. "Who do you say I am?" [16] *Simon Peter answered, "You are the Messiah, the Son of the living God."* [17]

— Matthew 16:15-16

Mark 8:29 and Luke 9:20 record Jesus asking the same question. [18] [19]

In all three cases, Peter, one of Jesus' closes followers, answer clearly: Jesus is the Messiah.

In John's Gospel, Jesus makes His identity unmistakable. John 14:6–7 recounts one such moment. Jesus declares His identity without confusion:

"Jesus answered, 'I am the way and the truth and the life. No one comes to the Father except through me. If you really know me, you will know my Father as well. From now on, you do know him and have seen him.'" [20]

— John 14:6-7

Jesus declares Himself as the way, the truth, and the life. Along with the declaration of His closest followers, He connects Himself to God in all fullness.

This invites us into a deeper understanding of who Jesus is and ushers in a deep question of faith. Who do I believe Jesus to be?

If Jesus is not fully God, as He claims, then His sacrifice has no saving power. But Jesus is fully God, and He desires a relationship with you.

At the beginning of the Book of John, we read another powerful statement that helps reveal our understanding of God's identity.

---

17 Ibid. Mt 16:15–16.
18 Ibid. Mk 8:29.
19 Ibid. Lk 9:20.
20 Ibid. Jn 14:6–7.

"In the beginning was the Word, and the Word was with God, and the Word was God. He was with God in the beginning. Through him all things were made; without him nothing was made that has been made. In him was life, and that life was the light of all mankind. The light shines in the darkness, and the darkness has not overcome it." [21]

— John 1:1-5

Verse 14 connects the dots for us, helping us to see the "Word" that is God and the "He" mentioned at the start of the chapter is in fact Jesus.

"The Word became flesh and made his dwelling among us. We have seen his glory, the glory of the one and only Son, who came from the Father, full of grace and truth." [22]

— John 1:14

Jesus is the Word.
Jesus is life.
Jesus is light; and, He cannot be overcome.
In Revelation, we read another declaration of Jesus' identity:

"Look, I am coming soon! My reward is with me, and I will give to each person according to what they have done. I am the Alpha and the Omega, the First and the Last, the Beginning and the End." [23]

— Revelation 22:12-13

Understanding who God is and trying to wrap our head around His fullness is no simple task. The Trinity can be a confusing doctrine and we may wrestle with it our entire lives. God is, by definition, unfathomable. Yet, He is relational and, as we read in 1 John 4, He is love.

---

[21] Ibid. Jn 1:1–5.
[22] Ibid. Jn 1:14.
[23] Ibid. Re 22:12–13.

As followers of Christ, one of the most simple things we can come to accept is the centrality of God's identity as love. If we learn nothing else from trying to wrap our heads around the question of who God is, perhaps it is best summed up in what 1 John 4:7-8 says:

"Dear friends, let us love one another, for love comes from God. Everyone who loves has been born of God and knows God. 8 Whoever does not love does not know God, because God is love." [24]

— *1 John 4:7-8*

Jesus came to rescue you. He died for you. He conquered death for you. He did it for love. He exists as alpha and omega, as beginning and end. He is eternal. He presents Himself to us in different manners, for various purposes. He is Father. He is Son. He is Spirit.

In Him, we are invited into a relationship of perfect love because, "God is love." [25]

Discussion Questions

- Who do you say that Jesus is?
- How does your answer to that question change your relationship with God?
- Who do you need to invite into a deeper relationship with Him?

---

[24] Ibid. 1 Jn 4:7–8.
[25] Ibid.

"Therefore Jesus said again, 'Very truly I tell you, I am the gate for the sheep. [8] All who have come before me are thieves and robbers, but the sheep have not listened to them. [9] I am the gate; whoever enters through me will be saved. They will come in and go out, and find pasture. [10] The thief comes only to steal and kill and destroy; I have come that they may have life, and have it to the full.'" [26]

— John 10:7-10

Two Paths

Where Do I Go When I Die?

So far, we have explored the story of the Bible. We learned that we have a Bible because Jesus' followers heard what He said, saw what He did, witnessed His life, His death, and then, miraculously, saw Him alive after His resurrection.

Those who experienced Jesus firsthand wanted to obey His commands. Understanding this helps us grasp not only what the Bible is but why it matters.

In the last chapter, we asked the question: Who is God?

We explored the Trinity and touched on its historical development. Specifically, we looked at how early Roman churches articulated this concept to explain Christianity in a polytheistic and pagan world.

The Trinity teaches us that God is One:

- God the Father is fully God.
- God the Son is fully God.

[26] Ibid. Jn 10:7–10.

- God the Holy Spirit is fully God.

It is impossible to fully comprehend. But what truly matters is how we respond to Jesus' question to His disciples: "Who do people say that I am?"

How we answer this question about Jesus defines who we believe God to be. In short, we are wise to always remember: "God is love." [27]

However, in exploring these heady concepts about God's identity, we ultimately come to a question that is far more personal: What happens when I die?

This is The End

Pondering death leads to a question that is far more personal.

Perhaps you have faced this question during a surgery or you worried about the loss of a loved one after a car accident. Maybe it was when you received difficult news from a doctor? At some point in our lives, we all find ourselves standing over the casket of a loved one, asking, "Why, God?" Yet in the quiet of your mind, another question undoubtedly arises: "When will that be me?"

Whether we face it in a moment of grief, despair, or in an unexpected moment forced upon us, we each reach a final end to our life. The hard truth is simple: every person dies. Ten out of ten.

So the question before us is unavoidable:

What happens when we die?

The Bible is clear. There are two eternal destinations: Heaven and Hell. Jesus, teaching lays out the binary option before us.

---

[27] Ibid. 1 Jn 4:7–8.

"Then they will go away to eternal punishment, but the righteous to eternal life." [28]

— *Matthew 25:46*

What happens after we die is concealed in some amount of mystery. However, we can learn about the two places Jesus speaks of by surveying the Scriptures.

Heaven is a place to spend eternity with God. The Bible teaches heaven is filled with perfection. We get a snapshot of heaven's perfect design in the final book of the Bible:

"And I heard a loud voice from the throne saying, 'Look! God's dwelling place is now among the people, and he will dwell with them. They will be his people, and God himself will be with them and be their God.' 'He will wipe every tear from their eyes. There will be no more death' " or mourning or crying or pain, for the old order of things has passed away.'" [29]

— *Revelation 21:3-4*

The other option for where we may spend eternity is far less perfect.

Hell is a place eternally separated from God. We learn it is a place filled with agony and despair. Revelation 20 explains it as eternal torment.

---

[28] Ibid. Mt 25:46.

[29] Ibid. Re 21:3–4.

"And the devil, who deceived them, was thrown into the lake of burning sulfur, where the beast and the false prophet had been thrown. They will be tormented day and night for ever and ever." [30]

— *Revelation 20:10*

Then, the writer of Revelation explains the Day of Judgement that happens before God restores all things to perfection. We read that after the final judgement:

"Then death and Hades were thrown into the lake of fire. The lake of fire is the second death. Anyone whose name was not found written in the book of life was thrown into the lake of fire." [31]

— *Revelation 10:14-15*

If we accept this truth about an eternal relationship connected to lasting connection or separation, we must wonder what separates one place from the other?

On the day we come to grips with our own mortality, wondering if we are taking our final breaths, we ask, "If this is the end, then what is next?" More importantly, we must wonder what we must do to avoid the far less desirable option.

What can we do to avoid the despair of death?

[30] Ibid. Re 20:10.

[31] Ibid. Re 20:14–15.

God Chooses to Rescue Us

As bleak as contemplating death may feel, the story of Scripture does not end in despair. Nor are we meant to live in fear of the end. At the very center of the Bible's message is a hope strong enough to confront death itself: life does not end in the grave, and history does not end in abandonment.

The truly great news, revealed most fully in the life, death, and resurrection of Jesus Christ, is that God chose to rescue us. Salvation is not humanity's idea or achievement; it is God's initiative. From beginning to end, the biblical story is not about human beings climbing their way to God, but about God continually turning toward humanity and inviting us to turn our hearts toward Him.

The Orientation of the Heart

To understand this rescue, it helps to think not in terms of location or distance, but orientation. God does not move closer or farther away. God is constant. What changes is the direction of the human heart.

Throughout Scripture, sin is not described merely as rule-breaking, but as turning away. It is a reorientation of the heart away from God's light and toward something else. Repentance, by contrast, literally means *to turn back*. Salvation is, therefore, the restoration of direction: hearts turned once again toward the source of life.

Scripture often describes this orientation using the imagery of path and light. God sets before humanity a way to walk and a light to follow. When the heart is turned toward God, the path is illuminated. When the heart turns away, the path grows dark, confusing, and destructive.

Two verses that help us see this pattern in God's message can be found rooted in the Old Testament writings:

"Your word is a lamp for my feet, a light on my path." [32]

— *Psalm 119:105*

'Turn to me and be saved, all you ends of the earth; for I am God, and there is no other. [33]

— *Isaiah 45:22*

This framework – heart, path, and light – helps us understand free will and why it matters, especially when we ask the ultimate question: *What happens when I die?* The answer Scripture gives is deeply connected to the direction our hearts are oriented in this life.

The History of the World

Adam and Eve: Turning from the Light

God placed Adam and Eve in the garden in perfect fellowship, their hearts fully oriented toward Him. They walked in God's presence, illuminated by His light (Genesis 1–2). Yet when they chose to distrust God's word, their hearts turned away. Shame entered, and darkness followed. Still, God did not abandon them. Even in judgment, He pursued them with a promise of rescue (Genesis 3:15).

Jesus later echoes this reality when He teaches that humanity loves darkness rather than light, not because the light is absent, but because hearts resist it (John 3:19–21).

Cain and Abel: A Heart Turned Inward

[32] Ibid. Ps 119:105.
[33] Ibid. Is 45:22.

Cain and Abel both approached God with offerings, but Cain's heart turned inward toward jealousy and resentment. That inward turn led him off the path and into violence (Genesis 4). Yet even then, God marked Cain. It was not to destroy him, but to preserve him. Mercy interrupted judgment.

Jesus would later teach that murder begins in the heart long before it reaches the hands (Matthew 5:21–22).

Noah and the World: Walking Toward the Light

As humanity descended further into corruption, Scripture tells us that Noah "walked with God" (Genesis 6:9). His heart remained oriented toward the light while the world turned away. Through the flood, an image later echoed in baptism, God both judged evil and preserved life. Even after Noah's failure, God remained faithful, continuing His plan through Noah's son, Shem (Genesis 9).

Jesus later describes salvation as entering through a narrow way that leads to life, while many choose a wider path that leads to destruction (Matthew 7:13–14).

Abraham: A Wavering but Returning Heart

God called Abram to step into the light and walk a new path (Genesis 12). Abram's heart sometimes faltered; he attempted to fulfill God's promise through his own strength. Yet God remained faithful, reorienting Abram's heart again and again, establishing a covenant grounded in grace rather than perfection. Even after Abram's mistakes, God offers Him grace. When Abram fully embraces God, God re-establishes His covenant, or promise with the man. Abram's transformation is so profound that God changes the man's name. Abram became known as Abraham, the father of the peoples of Israel (Genesis 17:1-8).

Jesus later teaches that faith is not self-generated effort, but trust in God's provision (John 6:28–29). Jesus later explains that He was sent to fulfill the promises made to Abraham, saying "... before Abraham was born, I am." (John 8:48-59). [34]

Isaac: Trust on the Path

When Abraham, as a very old man, was asked to offer his son Isaac in a sacrifice, the test revealed the direction of his heart. Though fearful, he continued walking forward, trusting God to provide light even when the path was unclear (Genesis 22). God intervened, revealing that He is not like false gods who demand death, but the God who provides life.

Jesus later declares, "I am the way and the truth and the life." [35] As He does, He identifies Himself as both path and provision (John 14:6).

Jacob and Esau: Wrestling Toward the Light

Jacob's life was marked by deception and broken relationships. Yet on the night he feared facing his brother, Jacob wrestled with God Himself. In that struggle, his heart was reoriented. God renamed him Israel, marking transformation through encounter (Genesis 32).

Jesus later teaches that persistent seeking (knocking, asking, wrestling) leads to transformation (Matthew 7:7–8).

Joseph: A Heart Anchored in God

Joseph's heart remained oriented toward God despite betrayal, slavery, and imprisonment. Though others meant harm, God used suffering to preserve life (Genesis 50:20). Joseph's forgiveness reflected a heart aligned with God's mercy.

Jesus would later call His followers to forgive in the same way they have been forgiven (Matthew 18:21–35).

---

[34] Ibid. Jn 8:58.

[35] Ibid. Jn 14:6.

Moses: Learning to Trust the Light

God called Moses to lead Israel out of bondage, yet Moses doubted, feared, and failed. Still, God guided him step by step, illuminating the path through signs, provision, and covenant (Exodus 3–20). Moses is considered the author of the first five books of the Bible and was used by God to deliver the people of Israel from slavery to freedom.

Jesus later assures His followers that the Spirit will guide them into all truth (John 16:13). Furthermore, Jesus teaches us that He sets us completely free from the bondage and slavery of sin. (John 8:31-47).

Saul and David: Hearts Compared

Saul's heart slowly turned away, oriented toward fear and power. David, though deeply flawed, repeatedly turned his heart back toward God in repentance (1 Samuel and 2 Samuel). God chose David not for perfection, but for a heart aligned toward Him.

Jesus later teaches that God looks beyond outward appearances to the heart (Luke 16:15). He confronts the hypocrites, people who say one thing and do another, by calling out their inauthentic ways of life (Matthew 23).

Jesus: God as the Light

In Jesus, God Himself stepped into human history.

"In him was life, and that life was the light of all mankind. The light shines in the darkness, and the darkness has not overcome it."[36]

— John 1:4-5

[36] Ibid. Jn 1:4–5.

Jesus came as light, yet many turned away. The cross stands both as humanity's ultimate rejection, and as God's ultimate act of love. Through resurrection, Jesus revealed that even death cannot extinguish the light.

Jesus declares plainly:

"... he said, "I am the light of the world. Whoever follows me will never walk in darkness, but will have the light of life." [37]

— *John 8:12*

The Disciples and Paul: Hearts Reoriented

The disciples, those who followed Jesus during His ministry on Earth, sometimes doubted and denied Him. Paul, the Apostle who wrote the majority of the New Testament, even persecuted the church before following Jesus. Yet, in each case, Jesus pursued them all. Jesus sought to reorient their hearts and to send them out as witnesses. Through them, the light spread to the nations (Acts 1–9).

Jesus had promised this very work in the Great Commission, His final words before ascending to Heaven (Matthew 28:18-29 and Acts 1:7-11).

Martin Luther and the Church

As the church became entangled with power and corruption, hearts drifted from the light. God raised reformers like Martin Luther to call the church back to Scripture and grace, reorienting hearts toward Christ rather than control (Romans 1:17).

Jesus warned that religious structures could obscure truth if hearts were far from God (Matthew 15:8–9). Today, the church exists in fragments of denominational differences; however, they all agree on the Divinity of Jesus Christ and continue the work of reformation.

---

[37] Ibid. Jn 8:12b.

God and Me. God and You.

In my own life, God called me early. As a child I remember feeling a deep longing to pursue a relationship with Him. However, I gave into the temptations of what the world had to offer. I turned away, choosing my own path. Thankfully, God never stopped shining His light. Over time, He reoriented my heart. He did not approach me through force, but through grace. Even in my failures, stumbling off of the path in the dark, He invited me back into His love.

And now the question remains; a question that is deeply personal.

Where is your heart oriented today?

Some have turned away. Some once walked in the light but have drifted. Yet God remains where He has always been. Even today, He is calling, illuminating, inviting.

Revelation 3:20 tells us of the personal relationship He desires to have with each of us.

"Here I am! I stand at the door and knock. If anyone hears my voice and opens the door, I will come in and eat with that person, and they with me."[38]

— *Revelation 3:20*

The message of Jesus Christ is absolutely clear.

He desires to rescue you.

To redeem your family.

To heal your relationships.

He is and always has been: the light that shines and the path that is open.

Today, His invitation remains.

As the words of one Old Testament prophet remind us, He wants us to return to Him.

---

[38] Ibid. Re 3:20.

"Ever since the time of your ancestors you have turned away from my decrees and have not kept them. Return to me, and I will return to you," says the Lord Almighty." [39]

— *Malachi 3:7*

What remains is not whether God is willing to welcome us back. Rather, the questions is whether we will turn our hearts toward Him and walk in the light He provides.

Invitation

If you have never made a decision to follow Jesus, to accept God's loving invitation to be reunited with Him, let this be the moment. Accept that He has always and will always intervene on your behalf. He is seeking you. Will you seek Him?

Discussion Questions

- When is a time God intervened on your behalf and rescued you from yourself?
- Who do you need to tell about what you experienced? Why?
- Who is someone in your life that you can be praying for to accept God's forgiveness?

---

[39] Ibid. Mal 3:7.

"As a prisoner for the Lord, then, I urge you to live a life worthy of the calling you have received. Be completely humble and gentle; be patient, bearing with one another in love. Make every effort to keep the unity of the Spirit through the bond of peace. There is one body and one Spirit, just as you were called to one hope when you were called; one Lord, one faith, one baptism; one God and Father of all, who is over all and through all and in all. [40]

— *Ephesians 4:1-6*

One Faith

What Must I Do to Be Saved?

Asking the Difficult Questions

Considering the history of the world and the binary options of our eternity (heaven OR hell) we now must ask one of the most important questions a person can ask: What must I do to be saved?

Another way to frame this question is: *What must I do to experience deliverance from my sin and its consequences?*

Why Must I Be Saved?

To answer this, let's start with asking "Why?" *Why must I be saved?*

The question behind this question is connected to last chapter and is made urgently important when we ponder: *What happens when I die?* These questions work together to reveal the urgency of the message of salvation.

[40] Ibid. Eph 4:1–6.

We must be saved because:

- We have a sinful and rebellious nature that is self-seeking
    - Romans 3:10-12 & 23, Ephesians 2:1-3, Galatians 5:19-21, Philippians 2:21
- We have been given free will and the opportunity to decide.
    - Matthew 23:37, John 7:17, Romans 10:9-10, Revelation 3:20, 2 Corinthians 5:20
- We get to choose to accept or reject God's love.
    - John 3:16-19, John 1:11-12, Acts 7:51, Hebrews 3:7-8, Matthew 7:21

When we consider the existence of an eternity in either heaven or hell, and the nature of our freedom to choose, we have to make a decision. The choice we make about who we believe Jesus Christ to be will determine where we spend eternity. Simply put, the Bible makes it clear that every human being has failed, except for Jesus. Every human being needs salvation, provided through the grace of God in Jesus Christ.

Simply put: we must be saved because we are sinners. We continue in our sin until we surrender to God.

In Romans 3:21–26, Paul writes about the opportunity we have in Jesus Christ to be made right. The following text is from *The Message* and it captures the heart of the matter in way that is very approachable.

[21–24] But in our time something new has been added. What Moses and the prophets witnessed to all those years has happened. The God-setting-things-right that we read about has become Jesus-setting-things-right for us. And not only for us, but for everyone who believes in him. For there is no difference between us and them in this. Since we've compiled this long and sorry record as sinners (both us and them) and proved that we are utterly incapable of living the glorious lives God wills for us, God did it for us. Out of sheer generosity he put us in right standing with himself. A pure gift. He got us out of the mess we're in and restored us to where he always wanted us to be. And he did it by means of Jesus Christ.

[25–26] God sacrificed Jesus on the altar of the world to clear that world of sin. Having faith in him sets us in the clear. God decided on this course of action in full view of the public—to set the world in the clear with himself through the sacrifice of Jesus, finally taking care of the sins he had so patiently endured. This is not only clear, but it's now—this is current history! God sets things right. He also makes it possible for us to live in his rightness. [41]

— Romans 3:21-26 (MSG)

In summary, all have sinned. All have fallen short. Yet whether you are new to God or have known Him your whole life, we are each justified by God's grace through Christ Jesus. That is why salvation is necessary.

How Salvation Changes Us

[41] *Eugene H. Peterson, The Message: The Bible in Contemporary Language (Colorado Springs, CO: NavPress, 2005), Ro 3:21–26.*

The word "salvation" has deep meaning here. Simply put, salvation means "wholeness. and safety"; it can refer to "rescue from enemies" and "physical danger" or "restoration to wholeness in the kingdom of God." [42]

Salvation is often thought of in the Western world as deeply individualistic. But the reality is far richer:

- Salvation impacts our eternal destiny, yes, but it also transforms our current, earthly lives.
- It changes our friendships, marriages, parenting, work, and every relationship.
- Without salvation, we experience a type of hell on earth: brokenness, conflict, greed, selfishness, and generational harm.

When we are brought into the fullness of salvation, we often use the phrase: "I am saved." However, in the simplification, we sometimes miss the deeper experience of unity, love, and peace. When we completely experience salvation, it is a communalistic experience. We join other believers in the fullness of life that God intends.

Paul emphasizes this communal aspect repeatedly. A survey of Paul's letters to the churches reminds us that salvation allows us to:

- Know God and one another

---

[42] σωτηρία (*sōtēria*). n. fem. **salvation, wholeness, safety.** *Can refer to salvation from enemies, but in the nt is usually used of salvation from sin and death through Christ.*
This noun is related to σῴζω (*sōzō*, "to save") and means salvation, wholeness, and safety. In the Septuagint, *sōtēria* and the closely related word σωτήριος (*sōtērios*, "salvation") are the usual translations of the Hebrew יְשׁוּעָה (*yĕšûʿâ*, "salvation"), יֵשַׁע (*yēšaʿ*, "salvation"), and תְּשׁוּעָה (*tĕšûʿâ*, "salvation"), including when these words refer to military victory and rescue from enemies. In the nt, *sōtēria* can refer to rescue from enemies and other physical dangers (e.g., Luke 1:71; Heb 11:7; Acts 27:34) and to salvation from sins (e.g., Luke 1:77). Often, in the nt, the noun refers to rescue from sin and death through Christ and restoration to wholeness in the kingdom of God (e.g., Acts 4:12; Rom 1:16; Eph 1:13; 1 Pet 1:5; Rev 12:10).
Source: Joel T. Hamme, "Salvation," in *Lexham Theological Wordbook*, ed. Douglas Mangum et al., Lexham Bible Reference Series (Bellingham, WA: Lexham Press, 2014).

- Ephesians 1:17-18 and Philippians 1:9-10
- Live in peace
  - Romans 12:18 and Colossians 3:15
- Lead, serve, and bear one another's burdens
  - Galatians 6:2 and Ephesians 4:11-12
- Encourage and love one another
  - 1 Thessalonians 5:11 and Romans 12:10

Throughout his letters, Paul consistently teaches that salvation draws believers into a shared life where they grow in knowing God and one another, live in peace, serve humbly, bear burdens together, and build each other up in love. This is the nature of complete salvation, it changes us and every relationship we experience.

The New Testament guides us in learning to live this out. It reminds us of one truth: there is one message, one Word, one Lord, one baptism, one Church. Becoming saved aligns us with God's oneness and with His work in the world.

"As a prisoner for the Lord, then, I urge you to live a life worthy of the calling you have received. Be completely humble and gentle; be patient, bearing with one another in love. Make every effort to keep the unity of the Spirit through the bond of peace. There is one body and one Spirit, just as you were called to one hope when you were called; one Lord, one faith, one baptism; one God and Father of all, who is over all and through all and in all."[43]

— *Ephesians 4:1-6*

In choosing to follow Jesus, we are called into both a personal relationship and one that is communal. We are united with every other believer as we are joined in oneness with God. In this, we learn the deeper meaning of salvation.

---

[43] *The New International Version* (Grand Rapids, MI: Zondervan, 2011), Eph 4:1–6.

Salvation and The Church

So, what must we do to be saved? The Bible teaches a clear path through Jesus Christ. Different churches emphasize, or de-emphasize, particular passages to bring people into a relationship with Christ. Part of belonging to a local church is learning, and agreeing with your church's beliefs. Most churches have a statement of faith on their website or some document that lays out "What we believe."

My encouragement, as an author and as the pastor of a local church, is that you should always review those documents. Then, have a conversation with one of the pastors or leaders of your church to fully understand.

There are a lot of disagreements in scholarly circles about what is considered, or recognized as a denomination. The Church, collectively speaking, has a history full of division. In the past, these different belief systems could be distinguished by theology, nationality, and even race. Nowadays, as Steven Wedgeworth explains in a very well resourced article for Logos:

"People are less likely to choose a church based upon formal denominational affiliation and instead look for specific congregations based on social and political factors. The most notable dividing lines have become a church's belief about Scripture and ethics concerning sexuality, including both the relationship and roles between the sexes and the definition of marriage." [44]

— *Steven Wedgeworth*

[44] Wedgeworth, Steven. "The Definitive Guide to Christian Denominations." Word by Word, October 27, 2023. https://www.logos.com/grow/christian-denominations.

Most differences fall into categories originating from historical moments where interpretations, and the application of such, caused disagreements. This is, ultimately, good news because there are a plethora of churches offering many opportunities to worship, serve, and grow alongside of others who experience God in ways similar to you.

For example, if you prefer a more traditional approach to church, you might opt for one of the older denominations such as Catholicism, Orthodoxy, Lutheranism, or Anglican. If your preference is for a more emotionally charged experience, the Pentecostal churches will probably appeal to you more. For those of you who love modern worship and practical applications, the non-denominational churches (and some branches of the Baptist church) might make you feel at home.

If you are new to your faith, and unsure of where you should start, check out some online services of the churches nearest your home to see if they are the right fit. Then, visit in person and have an open mind and heart to grow. Each church is a little bit different because people are incredibly diverse.

Despite the differences and division, churches that are considered to be Christian do have central things in common with one another. At "the core of any genuine Christian denomination is the belief that Jesus Christ is the son of God and that anyone putting their trust and faith in him is forgiven by God." [45]

Whatever you do, test out the church's commitment to Scripture and find out who they believe Jesus Christ to be. If the church is unwilling to have hard conversations about how their beliefs align with God's Word, that's a warning sign and you should keep looking for the right fit. Sometimes it takes time to find the right church home.

---

[45] Christianity. "Different Denominations, Same God." Accessed January 30, 2026. https://www.christianity.org.uk/article/different-denominations-same-god-1.

For example, when I was growing up, I attended church at a United Methodist congregation at a tiny country church near our farm. As a young adult, my wife and I would sometimes visit the local Assemblies of God, a pentecostal church. When I came to my faith, it was through the radio ministry of Harvest Christian Fellowship, a member of the Calvary Chapel movement. In the United States Marines, my wife and I attended a chapel on base led by a Southern Baptist preacher. After I was honorably discharged from the Marines, we joined a Christian Church in my hometown of Corydon, Indiana. Later, as a missionary, I developed an online network connecting people across all manner of denominations and served them without prejudice.

God used the diversity of His body, the local church, to communicate to me His perfect love. If you had a bad experience at the church you grew up in, or at the one you recently attended, try another one. It is ok if necessary and a blessing once you find the right fit for you and your family.

Steps of Salvation

I share the winding road of my personal journey because it comes full circle back to the steps of salvation. Again, different churches emphasize, or de-emphasize, certain Scriptures to communicate to people their understanding of God's Word. These subtle difference can cause division, especially when we fall into legalism and intolerance. Unity with your local church will help you discern and work out your salvation.

In my faith tradition, as an ordained pastor in the Christian Church, we use a simple five step illustration to help explain salvation from the Bible. It originated during the Second Great Awakening through a historical movement known as the Restoration Movement. A frontier pastor, a man by the name of Walter Scott, coined the Five-Finger Gospel as a means of simplifying what the Bible teaches us to provide assurance of salvation. [46]

Scott's Five-Finger Gospel includes the following five steps:

1. Hear
2. Believe
3. Confession
4. Repentance
5. Baptism

Hear

The first step comes from hearing the Word of God. By extension, this means we must be open to hear and willing to tell others. Being connected to a local church is vital. Hearing God's Word brings repentance for the unbeliever and growth for the believer.

Paul writes about this in Romans 10:17:

"Consequently, faith comes from hearing the message,and the message is heard through the word about Christ." [47]

— *Romans 10:17*

[46] Stoned-Campbell Disciple. "Walter Scott and the Origins of the Five Finger Gospel." March 19, 2009. https://stonedcampbelldisciple.com/2009/03/19/walter-scott-and-the-origins-of-the-five-finger-gospel/.

[47] The New International Version (Grand Rapids, MI: Zondervan, 2011), Ro 10:17.

Believe

Hearing the Word brings us to a moment of decision. We must choose if we will accept it or reject it. Do we believe? Belief is the choice to trust in Jesus as Lord.

Acts 16:29–31, brings clarity to this moment through the eyes of a man seeking to "be saved."

"The jailer called for lights, rushed in and fell trembling before Paul and Silas. He then brought them out and asked, 'Sirs, what must I do to be saved?'

They replied, 'Believe in the Lord Jesus, and you will be saved—you and your household.'" [48]

— *Acts 16:29-31*

Confession

We also learn from the Bible that the act of confession is an important moment in experiencing salvation. Confession involves acknowledging our sin and God's Lordship over us.

To confess, we must come to grips with what is written in Romans 3:

"As it is written:

'There is no one righteous, not even one; there is no one who understands; there is no one who seeks God. All have turned away, they have together become worthless; there is no one who does good, not even one.' [49]

…

[23] *for all have sinned and fall short of the glory of God."* [50]

---

[48] Ibid. Ac 16:29–31.
[49] Ibid. Ro 3:10–12.
[50] Ibid. Ro 3:23.

— *Romans 3:10-12 and 23*

Later in Romans, we read that this sin nature, our fallen and rebellious state, carries a cost:

"For the wages of sin is death…"

— *Romans 6:23a*

The verse then continues with a message of hope through Jesus Christ, teaching us:

"... but the gift of God is eternal life in Christ Jesus our Lord." [51]

— *Romans 6:23b*

This message of hope in Jesus, despite our rebellion, permeates Scripture. Consider, one such instance, also from the Book of Romans:

"But God demonstrates his own love for us in this:

While we were still sinners, Christ died for us." [52]

— *Romans 5:8*

A powerful passage revealing the need for confession comes from 1 John:

"If we claim to be without sin, we deceive ourselves and the truth is not in us. [9] If we confess our sins, he is faithful and just and will forgive us our sins and purify us from all unrighteousness." [53]

— *1 John 1:8-9*

---

[51] Ibid. Ro 6:23.
[52] Ibid. Ro 5:8.
[53] Ibid. 1 Jn 1:8–9.

Repentance

Repentance follows confession and it means turning away from sin and pursuing God. It is a rejection of our self and a soul-deep acceptance of Christ.

Jesus taught repentance and He clearly instructed His disciples to teach the same. For example, when He dispatches His disciples to share His message, we read in Mark's Gospel:

12 They went out and preached that people should repent. [54]

— Mark 6:12

We also read, throughout the Book of Acts, that the early church taught a turning away from sin (repentance) as part of the message of Jesus. A great example of this teaching comes from chapter three:

"Repent, then, and turn to God, so that your sins may be wiped out, that times of refreshing may come from the Lord…" [55]

— Acts 3:19

God calls us each to reject our default state of fallenness and to turn back to God.

---

[54] Ibid. Mk 6:12.

[55] Ibid. Ac 3:19.

Baptism

Baptism is a public declaration of the choice to follow Jesus Christ.

It is worth noting here the oddly divisive way churches teach baptism. Some churches teach it is required for salvation. They legalistically insist you must be an adult and it must be by immersion. Others teach it is completely option and merely symbolic. There is every mix of interpretation that lies between those two extremes.

To some churches, it carries the heavy equivalent of a marriage ceremony and is required for membership. To others, you can be sprinkled, even as an infant, to be considered baptized.

In my studies of the New Testament, I have found wisdom in submitting myself into agreement with what I read in the Scriptures. Generally speaking, the pattern we see, after Jesus' ascension, is that every time someone experiences salvation they are baptized by immersion. Therefore, this implies the early church learned the teachings of Baptism from Jesus and taught it as part of the message of salvation.

True, there is no verse in the Bible that says baptism is required for salvation. I am in agreement with this as well. However, as a pastor called to teach what the Bible teaches, I always include baptism because, through extracting truth from God's Word, it appears to me it was taught by those who spent time directly with Jesus. The example set in the early church is enough reason for me to include it. At the same time, God's grace abounds and His love is not legalistic. I teach baptism but also hold to the notion that God's grace is always enough to save.

In short, I feel required to teach baptism because of what the Bible teaches. Based on the Scriptures, and the authority of your local church, you need to wrestle with your own understanding to decide if you feel baptism is necessary. It is ultimately between you and God.

One place in Scripture we see baptism taught as a part of salvation comes from an early moment in the first century church's history. A large crowd is gathered and they ask the Apostle Peter what they must do.

"Peter replied, 'Repent and be baptized, every one of you, in the name of Jesus Christ for the forgiveness of your sins. And you will receive the gift of the Holy Spirit. 39 The promise is for you and your children and for all who are far off—for all whom the Lord our God will call.'" [56]

— Acts 2:38-39

Again, the New Testament consistently and routinely includes baptism as a part of the message of salvation (Acts 8:36, 9:18, 16:33, and Romans 6:1-14). It also teaches us that grace is enough to save in Romans 3:21-22 and 28:

"But now apart from the law the righteousness of God has been made known, to which the Law and the Prophets testify. This righteousness is given through faith in Jesus Christ to all who believe."

...

"For we maintain that a person is justified by faith apart from the works of the law." [57]

— Romans 3:21-22 and 28

---

[56] Ibid. Ac 2:38–39.

[57] Ibid. Ro 3:21-23 & 28.

My goal here is not to convince you of one perspective or the other, that is outside the scope of this book. However, I do urge you to talk to your local church about it, pray to God for wisdom, and seek the Scriptures so that you can have full assurance and experience peace in your relationship with God.

The Result of Salvation

Responding to God's Word in obedience leads to an assurance that grants us peace, justification, and love (Romans 5:1, 8:1-2, and 12:9-21). This is the result of salvation. Salvation transforms both personal and communal life.

We become united with Christ and are then commanded to become love in action.

Prayer for Salvation

After reading this, if you desire salvation and do not know where to start, start with a prayer. You can pray this prayer:

"Father in heaven, I praise you for your good and perfect love.

Please forgive me for my sins. I believe your Word to be true. I confess my need for a Savior. I admit I am a sinner and I need your love.

Thank you for the free gift of salvation through Jesus.

Thank you for the freedom to choose You.

Help me to be a light to others, to live out Your love in my family, community, work, and everywhere.

Help me to find a local church where I can grow in the Way of Jesus Christ.

Help me to follow You and teach others about You.

I choose You as my Lord and Savior and give my life completely to You.

Amen."

If you prayed that prayer, and you need help with your next steps or would just like to share what you are experiencing with someone, I urge you to start by telling the people closest to you. Share it with those you care most about.

Additionally, it would be a great joy to me to hear some of your story. Email me: me@michaeljchanley.com. I'd love to hear from you!

Living Salvation in Community

When salvation is lived out, even imperfectly, it produces unity in our lives. We experience unity in our heart, our home, and in the Church.

Paul writes in his letter to the church in Ephesus:

"As a prisoner for the Lord, then, I urge you to live a life worthy of the calling you have received. Be completely humble and gentle; be patient, bearing with one another in love. Make every effort to keep the unity of the Spirit through the bond of peace. There is one body and one Spirit, just as you were called to one hope when you were called; one Lord, one faith, one baptism; one God and Father of all, who is over all and through all and in all." [58]

— Ephesians 4:1-6

In oneness, we begin to experience the complete joy of our salvation.

---

[58] Ibid. Eph 4:1–6.

When we live with complete humility and patience, when we live with gentleness and love, when we live in the Spirit, together as one body, we begin to experience a faith that is sincere and authentic. On the surface, this looks like a local church fully committed to being a reflection of Jesus Christ in the world. It is the essence of every Christian church: a community of believers living out the love and unity of Christ.

As we close this chapter, I want to just take a moment to encourage you to honor those who have chosen to serve in our church community. These individuals (pastors, ministers, elders, deacons, overseers, leaders) exemplify what it means to live out salvation in action. They offer their time, talent, and love to make the body of Christ strong and vibrant.

When you reach out to them to talk about your faith, or to ask questions about what your church believes, let them know you encourage them. Pursue a conversation in unity and always keep love at the center of all you do.

Discussion Questions

- Will you practice using the Five-Finger Gospel to explain the steps of salvation: Hear, Believe, Confess, Repent, Be Baptized, and receive Eternal Life?
- How is this simple tool still relevant and useful in our world today?
- Who could you share the steps of salvation with this week?

These questions are meant to guide your reflection and encourage you to live out the truths of this chapter, not just in your personal life, but within your family, community, and church.

"Have nothing to do with godless myths and old wives' tales; rather, train yourself to be godly. For physical training is of some value, but godliness has value for all things, holding promise for both the present life and the life to come. This is a trustworthy saying that deserves full acceptance. That is why we labor and strive, because we have put our hope in the living God, who is the Savior of all people, and especially of those who believe." [59]

…

"Be diligent in these matters; give yourself wholly to them, so that everyone may see your progress. Watch your life and doctrine closely. Persevere in them, because if you do, you will save both yourself and your hearers.: [60]

— 1 Timothy 4:7-10 & 15-16

No Worries

This book has sought to address the foundational aspects of the Christian faith, providing clarity on what it means to follow Jesus and live in alignment with His teachings. Some of what has been shared may be familiar to those who have grown up in the church; for others, it may be entirely new. In either case, the essential truth remains the same: now you know, and this knowledge calls for action.

Christianity is not merely a set of beliefs to be held quietly, but a life to be lived.

[59] Ibid. 1 Ti 4:7–10

[60] Ibid. 1 Ti 4:15–16.

Through reflection and study, many have found encouragement and guidance in understanding how faith interacts with daily life. Theology can be complex, but it is foundational. The work of understanding and internalizing these truths provides a solid foundation for living, growing, and serving in the world.

What Does It Mean to Be a Christian?

To be a Christian is often misunderstood in the world. Cultural misconceptions can attach judgment, oppression, or prejudice to the label. Yet, these are the opposite of Christ's teaching.

The word "Christian" itself reveals a deeper truth. The first followers of Jesus were called Christians in Antioch (Acts 11:26). The term likely began as an insult, reflecting the lowly status, outsider position, and perceived impurity of those early believers. Some scholars suggest it even meant "the oily ones," referring to the appearance of people who labored under harsh conditions.

Over time, however, the early Christians embraced the term. They acknowledged their humility, their lowly status, and, most importantly, their total submission to Christ. The term "Christian" therefore carries two complementary meanings: to be Christ-like and to be a slave of Christ. [61]

Being a slave to Christ is central to the Christian life. It means willingly submitting to God's authority, rejecting the ways of the world, and living in accordance with His truth and love. Paul's letter to the Romans expresses this beautifully:

---

[61] Dickie, J. (1915). Christian. In J. Orr, J. L. Nuelsen, E. Y. Mullins, & M. O. Evans (Eds.), *The International Standard Bible Encyclopaedia* (Vol. 1–5, p. 622). Chicago: The Howard-Severance Company.

"But now that you have been set free from sin and have become slaves of God, the benefit you reap leads to holiness, and the result is eternal life. For the wages of sin is death, but the gift of God is eternal life in Christ Jesus our Lord. [62]

— Romans 6:22-23

To be a Christian is not to wield power over others but to submit to the Master who sets the path of life. It is a life defined by service, love, humility, and surrender.

Growing in Christlikeness

The question then arises: how do we grow in Christlikeness? One helpful framework comes from Richard Foster's *Celebration of Discipline*, which identifies three movements of the Spirit: Inward, Outward, and Corporate Disciplines. [63]

The inward disciplines are meditation, prayer, fasting, study. These practices allow for self-examination, personal transformation, and intimacy with God.

The outward disciplines are simplicity, solitude, submission, service.

These shape our interaction with the world, helping us to live in a way that reflects God's love.

The corporate disciplines are confession, worship, guidance, celebration.

These cultivate a sense of community, drawing us closer to both God and one another.

Practicing these disciplines gradually transforms character and aligns the life of the believer with the example of Christ. The spiritual disciplines are, at their core, about intentionality. It is a dying to the self in pursuit of formation in Christ.

---

[62] *The New International Version* (Grand Rapids, MI: Zondervan, 2011), Ro 6:22–23.

[63] Foster, Richard J. *Celebration of Discipline: The Path to Spiritual Growth*. Rev. ed. San Francisco: Harper, 1988.

An Illustration of the Disciplines

Consider a simple example from everyday life. In tending a garden and caring for bees, one can find moments of solitude, simplicity, and awe. Observing the bees, feeling the grass beneath one's feet, and reflecting on God's creation becomes an act of worship and celebration. Such moments offer space for God to speak, clarify calling, and nurture faith.

In this way, spiritual disciplines cultivate the growth of a life that follows Christ, opening the heart to service, love, and obedience. They prepare the believer to act courageously and faithfully, guided by the Spirit.

This Is Basic Christianity

At its core, Christianity is faith grounded in the Bible and the life, death, and resurrection of Jesus. It is faith that seeks to answer three essential questions:

1. Who is God? God is one: Father, Son, and Holy Spirit, and God's nature is love. Jesus came as fully God and fully human to reconcile the world to God.
2. What happens when we die? Each individual faces a choice. Through free will, we may accept or reject God's salvation. Eternal life is offered to those who believe, repent, and follow Christ. Our choice affects us individually and the people we most care about.
3. What must we do to be saved? We hear the Word, believe, confess our sins, repent, and publicly demonstrate our faith, often starting with (or including) baptism. These acts signify death to self and resurrection in Christ, bringing transformation and the power to love and serve others.

To be a Christian is to allow God's love to shine through us. It is to serve those who are marginalized, lost, or enslaved to sin, reflecting God's mercy in every interaction. It moves us to both compassion and empathy.

Jesus teaches a new command that becomes proof positive of our commitment to Him. In John we read:

"A new command I give you: Love one another. As I have loved you, so you must love one another. By this everyone will know that you are my disciples, if you love one another." [64]

—John 13:34-35

Following Jesus means love is no longer an option. It is a command. Love becomes our rule of life and the default mode of the believer.

Living Without Worry

To live as a Christian is to reject the slavery of the world and embrace the freedom of submission to Christ. True freedom is found not in autonomy, but in surrender to God. It brings peace, purpose, and the ability to rise above life's trials. In Christ, believers are empowered to love unconditionally, act courageously, and live without fear.

This is the essence of Basic Christianity: a life rooted in the Word of God, submitted to Christ, and lived in obedience and love. To be a Christian is to be a slave to Christ, growing daily in His likeness, and allowing His love to transform not only oneself but also the world around us.

---

[64] *The New International Version* (Grand Rapids, MI: Zondervan, 2011), Jn 13:34–35.

Discussion Questions

- What is a spiritual discipline which comes easy for you?
- Which ones do you find to be the most difficult?
- Discuss why you answered the above questions and how you can encourage others to grow in your faith through practicing one of the spiritual disciplines together.

Living as a Christian is a journey of surrender, transformation, and service. It is a life that reflects Christ in thought, word, and action. It is a life that allows God's perfect love to flow through every part of existence. As one grows in Christlikeness, the influence of that life spreads, impacting family, community, and the world. This is the enduring invitation of Basic Christianity: to follow Christ fully, serve Him faithfully, and live a life of love that bears witness to His truth.

Essentials of Basic Christianity

The following outline provides an overview of what has been covered in this book.

1. Understanding God
    a. God is one: Father, Son, and Holy Spirit.
    b. God's nature is love. Jesus came fully God and fully human to reconcile the world to God.

2. The Meaning of Salvation
    a. Salvation is God's intervention in our lives, rescuing us from sin and eternal separation.
    b. Steps to salvation:
        i. Hear the Word of God.
        ii. Believe in Jesus Christ.
        iii. Confess sin and acknowledge Christ as Lord.
        iv. Repent and turn from old ways.
        v. Baptism as a public sign of faith and transformation.
    c. Salvation transforms both personal life and the world around us.

3. What It Means to Be a Christian
    a. A Christian is a follower and a servant of Christ, a "slave of God."
    b. This means submitting to God's authority, rejecting worldly systems of sin, and living in obedience and love.
    c. Christianity is not about judgment or power over others; it is about reflecting God's unconditional love.

4. Spiritual Growth and Discipline
    a. Growth in Christ comes through spiritual disciplines, divided into three movements:
        i. Inward: meditation, prayer, fasting, study.
        ii. Outward: simplicity, solitude, submission, service.
        iii. Corporate: confession, worship, guidance, celebration.
    b. Practicing these disciplines transforms character, aligns life with God's will, and strengthens community.

5. Living in Christlikeness
    a. The goal of the Christian life is to become more like Jesus.
    b. True freedom is found in surrender to God, not in worldly independence.
    c. Christlike living enables love, courage, and peace, allowing believers to rise above trials and bring God's light to others.

6. The Call to Action
    a. Now that you know these truths, act on them:
        i. Live your faith visibly and intentionally.
        ii. Serve others and extend God's love, especially to those who are marginalized or hurting.
        iii. Encourage one another in spiritual growth and accountability.
    b. Christianity is a journey of continual surrender, transformation, and service. It is a life that allows God's love to flow through us and change the world.

Sources

Christianity. "Different Denominations, Same God." Accessed January 30, 2026. https://www.christianity.org.uk/article/different-denominations-same-god-1.

Dickie, J. (1915). Christian. In J. Orr, J. L. Nuelsen, E. Y. Mullins, & M. O. Evans (Eds.), *The International Standard Bible Encyclopaedia* (Vol. 1–5, p. 622). Chicago: The Howard-Severance Company.

Eugene H. Peterson, The Message: The Bible in Contemporary Language (Colorado Springs, CO: NavPress, 2005), Ro 3:21–26.

Foster, Richard J. *Celebration of Discipline: The Path to Spiritual Growth*. Rev. ed. San Francisco: Harper, 1988.

Hudson, M. "Battle of Milvian Bridge." Encyclopedia Britannica, October 21, 2025. https://www.britannica.com/topic/Battle-of-the-Milvian-Bridge.

Joel T. Hamme, "Salvation," in *Lexham Theological Wordbook*, ed. Douglas Mangum et al., Lexham Bible Reference Series (Bellingham, WA: Lexham Press, 2014).

Kierkegaard, Soren. Provocations: Spiritual Writings of Kierkegaard. Plough Publishing House 2014., 2014.

Kings & Generals Channel on YouTube. *Milvian Bridge 312 - Rise of Christianity DOCUMENTARY*. Accessed January

30, 2026. https://www.youtube.com/watch?v=VbFtMXytMj8.

Larson, Eugene. *Japanese Ban Christian Missionaries* | Research Starters | EBSCO Research. Accessed January 29, 2026. https://www.ebsco.com.

Sanders, Fred. "Who Said 'The Trinity: Try to Understand It, and You'll Lose Your Mind'?" The Scriptorium Daily, August 30, 2009. https://scriptoriumdaily.com/who-said-the-trinity-try-to-understand-it-and-youll-lose-your-mind/.

Stoned-Campbell Disciple. "Walter Scott and the Origins of the Five Finger Gospel." March 19, 2009. https://stonedcampbelldisciple.com/2009/03/19/walter-scott-and-the-origins-of-the-five-finger-gospel/.

Strong, J. (2009). *A Concise Dictionary of the Words in the Greek Testament and The Hebrew Bible* (Vol. 1, p. 58). Bellingham, WA: Logos Bible Software.

Templar Cross. "In Signo Hoc Vinces: Meaning and Origin." July 31, 2020. https://templar-cross.com/blogs/knights-templar-blog/in-signo-hoc-vinces.

The New International Version. (2011). (2 Ti 3:10–17). Grand Rapids, MI: Zondervan.

Wedgeworth, Steven. "The Definitive Guide to Christian Denominations." Word by Word, October 27, 2023. https://www.logos.com/grow/christian-denominations/.

About the Author

Michael J. Chanley is a pastor, teacher, and writer with a deep passion for helping people understand God's love and live out their faith with clarity and purpose.

After honorably serving in the United States Marine Corps, Michael followed a calling into ministry that has spanned more than 25 years. During that time, he has served in a wide range of roles including local church leadership, executive leadership, global missions, and children's and family ministry. He currently serves as Pastor of Tunnel Hill Christian Church in Georgetown, Indiana, a community committed to growing in faith, sharing hope, and loving one another as followers of Jesus.

Michael holds a Master's degree in Ministry and Leadership from Lincoln Christian Seminary and bachelor's degrees in history and sociology. He is currently pursuing a Doctor of Ministry through Emmanuel Christian Seminary at Milligan University. He has also completed professional certificate programs through Harvard University.

He has been married to his wife, Rose, for over 30 years. Together they have three children and one grandson. They live on a small farm in southern Indiana, where they enjoy a slower pace of life alongside chickens, peafowl, a chocolate lab, far too many cats, and an apiary of honeybees.

Michael's books regularly appear on hot new release and bestseller lists. He speaks at a limited number of events each year. More information, speaking inquiries, and additional resources can be found at **michaeljchanley.com.**

Also from Michael J. Chanley

Hope & Honeybees: Lessons of Faith From a Local Beekeeper a study on the biblical theme of hope, with lessons extracted from the life of honeybees.

Escape:The Traps of Christianity an exploration in the pursuit of authentic Christianity.

Chasing Whales: A Spiritual Dive with Jonah an interactive resource designed to teach Bible study methods while diving deeply into the story of Jonah.

Please visit **michaeljchanley.com** for more details and to discover other available books and resources.

REDISCOVER GOD'S MESSAGE OF LOVE

BETTER TOGETHER

God Called Love: Experience Love In An Anxious World Needing Grace is an approachable approachable, thematic exploration of love from the Book of John. Focused on God's love, it challenges both the new believer and life long sojourner, to rediscover the heart of Jesus.

Experiencing God's Love: 5 Week Journal On God's Love & Spiritual Practices Guidebook builds on the theme of love and invites you into a week's long journey of spiritual growth.

Visit **michaeljchanley.com** to order your copies now and to discover other available books and resources.

www.ingramcontent.com/pod-product-compliance
Lightning Source LLC
LaVergne TN
LVHW090535110826
845146LV00003B/1115
9798989227761